CORDOBA CITY

TRAVEL GUIDE 2024

Unveiling Cordoba City: A Coastal Gem's,
Historic Wonders, Hidden Treasures and
Timeless Charms in 2024

Thomas A. Olvera

Table of Contents

1. INTRODUCTION

1.1 Welcome to Cordoba City

Cordoba City, nestled along the shore, shines as a beacon of historical riches and natural beauty, capturing the hearts of visitors from all over the world. As you travel through this coastal treasure, prepare to be enveloped in a tapestry of varied cultures, architectural wonders, and landscapes that effortlessly merge the ancient and the new.

1.2 Geographical Significance

Cordoba City's geographical setting is an important part of its beauty. Its seaside location provides a distinct blend of coastal influences and historical relevance. The city is strategically located, providing a gateway to the vast ocean while simultaneously serving as a hub of trade and cultural interaction throughout its long history. The surrounding scenery, ranging from gorgeous beaches to lush greenery, adds to the city's attraction.

1.3 What Makes Cordoba City Unique?

What distinguishes Cordoba City is its ability to perfectly blend a rich history with a dynamic current culture. The city's streets whisper stories of old civilizations, as evidenced by its architectural marvels and preserved historical districts. Meanwhile, Cordoba's modern pulse beats via its bustling markets, vibrant festivals, and avant-garde art scene. It's a site where tradition and innovation coexist, resulting in a unique environment that captivates every visitor.

Cordoba's uniqueness also stems from its people, who are noted for their kindness and hospitality. As you travel through the city, don't be shocked if locals meet you with a pleasant smile or offer stories about hidden jewels only known to Cordoba residents. Cordoba City is unique in that it combines historical significance, cultural richness, and welcoming residents.

1.4 Why visit Cordoba in 2024?

Cordoba has always been an attractive location, but 2024 offers unique potential. This year, the city is introducing new attractions, hosting interesting events, and providing unique experiences, making it a great opportunity to discover its delights.

In 2024, Cordoba's festivals and events guarantee an immersive cultural experience. The city's calendar is jam-packed with activities that cater to a wide range of interests, from historically significant anniversaries to cutting-edge art festivals. Imagine taking part in colorful street parades, sampling local specialties at food festivals, and seeing pioneering performances by artists from all over the world.

Furthermore, continuous restoration work has revitalized historical sites, allowing visitors to see the city's past in all its beauty. These attempts demonstrate Cordoba's commitment to conserving its legacy while embracing modernity, resulting in a vibrant tapestry that depicts the city's progress over time.

The year 2024 also marks the start of Cordoba's sustainable tourist activities. From eco-friendly lodgings to community-based tours, the city is promoting responsible tourism. Visitors in 2024 can contribute to these projects, which will benefit the environment and the local community.

Finally, Cordoba City beckons in 2024, promising to reveal its seaside wonders, historic treasures, and timeless charms in ways never seen before. Whether you're looking for cultural immersion, historical exploration, or simply the thrill of discovering hidden gems, Cordoba is ready to charm you with its allure. So pack your bags and prepare for a tour through a city that perfectly blends the past, present, and future into an unparalleled tapestry of experiences.

2. HISTORIC JOURNEY

2.1 Tracing Cordoba's Past

A historic excursion through Cordoba is like walking into a living history book. The city's roots go back thousands of years, and each cobblestone street tells a narrative about the civilizations that have thrived here. Tracing Cordoba's history is an intriguing journey that reveals the layers of history woven into the fabric of this seaside beauty.

Cordoba's history begins in the second century BC when the Carthaginians founded the city. The Romans, Visigoths, and Moors all left indelible traces on the city, influencing its architecture, culture, and character. The Roman Bridge, which stands majestically across the Guadalquivir River, is a tribute to ancient technical feats. It serves as a symbolic doorway into Cordoba's historical depths, inviting visitors to journey through time.

As you go through the city's labyrinthine streets, the Alcazar of Cordoba stands out as a living witness to the Moorish influence. Originally a stronghold, the Alcazar's exquisite Islamic design transports you to a bygone period, echoing the stories of caliphs and rulers who once trod among its walls. The centuries-long juxtaposition of Islamic art and Christian additions highlights Cordoba's complex cultural blend.

2.2 Historical Sites and Monuments

Cordoba's historic landscape is embellished with a variety of structures and monuments that serve as silent witnesses to the city's rich history. The Mezquita-Catedral is undoubtedly the crown treasure. This architectural masterpiece represents religious evolution, beginning as a mosque in the eighth century and subsequently becoming a cathedral during the Reconquista. The Mezquita's stunning horseshoe arches, intricate mihrab, and tall minaret represent the many cultural influences that have molded Cordoba throughout the years.

The Jewish Quarter, often known as Juderia, is another historical site. Its tiny, winding alleyways lead to the Cordoba Synagogue, one of Spain's few remaining medieval synagogues. This hallowed place, with its Mudejar and Gothic characteristics, provides a peek into the life of the once-thriving Jewish community in this area.

Moving on, the Calahorra Tower watches the Roman Bridge, serving as a quiet witness to the city's development. Its museum provides insights into Cordoba's history, as well as a panoramic perspective of the city's ancient foundations and current cityscape.

2.3 Walking Through Time: Heritage Trails

Cordoba allows history buffs to immerse themselves in its past via meticulously planned heritage routes. These pathways wind through the city's historic areas, revealing hidden gems and lesser-known sights that the casual spectator could miss.

The Cordoba Historic Center Trail takes you into the city's heart, where the architectural marvels of the Mezquita-Catedral, Alcazar, and Roman Temple stand out. Walking down these sacred routes, you can almost feel the echoes of past eras reverberating through the stones beneath your feet.

The Medieval Cordoba Trail, which snakes through the Jewish Quarter's small lanes, provides a more immersive experience. As you explore, you'll come across gorgeous patios, ancient fountains, and artisan workshops that have weathered the test of time. The walk culminates at the Alcazar, where visitors can view Cordoba's historic beauty.

In essence, wandering through time in Cordoba allows you to connect with the city's past in a more personal way. Each heritage route takes visitors on a trip through history, providing a detailed insight into the events, cultures, and people who created Cordoba into the enchanting city it is today.

Finally, Cordoba's historical voyage is a fascinating tour through the ages. From prehistoric civilizations to medieval splendors, the city's historic landmarks and historical trails provide a thorough examination of its rich and diverse history. So put on your walking shoes, let history guide you, and explore the layers of Cordoba's past that are waiting to be revealed around each corner.

3. PLANNING YOUR TRIP

To ensure a pleasant and enriching experience, plan your trip to Cordoba City carefully. From comprehending weather trends to navigating admission formalities, this thorough guide will provide you with all the information you need to make the most of your stay.

3.1 Weather and Best Time to Visit

Cordoba has a Mediterranean climate distinguished by scorching summers and moderate winters. The ideal seasons to visit, in terms of both weather and crowds, are spring (April to June) and fall (September to November). During these months, temperatures range from 15 to 25 degrees Celsius, making for a nice exploration atmosphere.

Summer (July-August) brings blazing temperatures that sometimes exceed 40 degrees Celsius. While this is perfect for sunbathers, it is critical to stay hydrated and schedule outdoor activities early in the morning or late in the afternoon to avoid the hottest hours.

Winter (December to February) brings cooler temperatures, ranging from 5 to 15 degrees Celsius. While it may not be as crowded, some outdoor attractions may have limited hours or require repair at this time. It is recommended that visitors check the specific opening times of attractions ahead of time.

3.2 Visa & Entry Requirements

Before visiting Cordoba, you should be aware of the visa and admission procedures. As of January 2022, Spain is a member of the Schengen Area, which allows nationals of numerous countries to enter without a visa for short periods (up to 90 days within 180 days). However, admission criteria can vary, so check with official government sources or the Spanish consulate for the most up-to-date information.

Make sure your passport is valid for at least six months after your scheduled departure date. Check to see if any specialized permits are required for activities like guided tours or special events.

3.3 Transportation Guide

Cordoba and its environs are easily navigated thanks to a well-connected transportation network. Cordoba Train Station serves the city, connecting it to major Spanish cities such as Madrid and Seville by high-speed AVE trains. The central bus terminal offers extra possibilities for regional travel.

Walking is one of the greatest methods to discover the city's historic areas. The compact architecture allows for easy transitions between attractions. Biking is also a popular and environmentally beneficial activity, with bike rental options accessible.

For a more immersive experience, consider taking public transportation or hiring a taxi. Cordoba's public transportation system is efficient and covers a variety of routes, making it easy to visit areas beyond the city center.

3.4 Budgeting and Costs

When budgeting for your vacation to Cordoba, you must consider accommodation, meals, transportation, and attractions. While Spain, in general, has a variety of options to suit all budgets, Cordoba's reputation as a tourist destination can influence rates.

Accommodation expenses vary, with options ranging from low-cost hostels to luxurious hotels. Consider lodging in the city center for convenient access to key attractions. Dining out is a pleasant experience in Cordoba, and visiting local tapas places can be both inexpensive and culturally enriching. Make room in your budget for unexpected discoveries and one-of-a-kind experiences.

Attraction prices may vary, and some locations provide discounts for students, the elderly, or certain time windows. Consider purchasing city passes or guided tour packages as a more cost-effective method to visit many attractions.

3.5 Communication and Internet Access

Cordoba's official language is Spanish, and while many inhabitants in tourist areas understand English, knowing a few basic Spanish phrases will help. Language applications and phrasebooks can be useful for communication.

Cordoba has a widespread internet connection, with hotels, cafes, and public locations offering free Wi-Fi. If you need continual connectivity, consider purchasing a local SIM card or an international data package for your smartphone.

3.6 Essential Travel Information

Understanding basic cultural conventions and local behaviors will help you enjoy your trip to Cordoba more. The Spanish siesta, a midday break during which many shops and businesses close, is still practiced in some areas. Plan your activities accordingly, and use this time for a leisurely lunch or a quiet siesta.

Tipping is expected in restaurants, and it is typical to round up the bill or leave a modest amount for excellent service. Cash is typically accepted, but credit cards are also popular.

Safety is not a major problem in Cordoba, but it is prudent to remain careful, particularly in popular tourist areas, and protect your goods against petty theft.

3.7 Packing Tips

When packing for a vacation to Cordoba, keep the season and intended activities in mind. Here are some key items to include:

1. For warm weather, wear lightweight, breezy clothing; for cooler evenings, layer.

2. Comfortable walking shoes for navigating the city's cobblestone streets.

3. To protect yourself from the sun, use sunscreen, sunglasses, and a hat.

4. A reusable water bottle helps you stay hydrated, especially during the hot summer months.

5. Adapters for electronic gadgets, as Spain mainly utilizes European standard (Type C) electrical outlets.

Consider bringing a small daypack with you on excursions to ensure you have essentials such as a map, guidebook, water, and any personal items you will need for the day.

Finally, when arranging a vacation to Cordoba, you must take into account a variety of aspects, ranging from weather to cultural habits. Armed with this knowledge, you can go on a journey that not only explores the city's historical wonders but also celebrates its rich culture and modern charm. With careful planning, your vacation to Cordoba promises to be a rewarding experience, leaving you with lasting memories of this seaside treasure.

4. ACCOMMODATION OPTIONS

Choosing the proper accommodations is an important part of arranging a successful and pleasurable vacation to Cordoba. The city, famed for its rich history and modern conveniences, provides a varied choice of hotel alternatives to suit a variety of interests and budgets. In this guide, we'll look at the various types of accommodations accessible, from deluxe hotels and resorts to low-cost stays and innovative lodging options that guarantee a great experience.

4.1 Hotel and Resort

Cordoba has several magnificent hotels and resorts that offer a pleasant escape for guests seeking comfort and indulgence. Many of these institutions are ideally positioned, providing easy access to the city's major attractions and cultural sites.

The Hospes Palacio del Bailío, a five-star hotel in a 16th-century palace, reflects the city's mix of history and luxury. With its lavish décor, beautiful gardens, and refreshing pool, it offers a peaceful haven in the middle of Cordoba.

For those looking for a resort experience, the Los Patios Hotel stands out with its gorgeous architecture and tranquil courtyard. This boutique hotel mixes modern conveniences with the elegance of classic Andalusian design, resulting in a distinct and charming atmosphere.

Staying in a hotel or resort in Cordoba frequently entails receiving exceptional services such as spa facilities, fine dining restaurants, and customized concierge help. The luxury and opulence of these lodgings add to the immersive experience, allowing guests to unwind and recharge after a day of seeing the city.

4.2 Budget-Friendly Stays

Cordoba understands the different demands of guests, and for those looking for more economical hotels, the city has a variety of options that do not sacrifice comfort or location.

Hostels like the Hostal Osio offer a cost-effective option for backpackers and budget-conscious travelers. These hostels, which are often located in the heart of the historic district, frequently provide both dormitory-style and private rooms, creating a sociable atmosphere for those wishing to connect with other tourists.

Guesthouses and boutique hotels, like La Llave de la Judería, offer a more customized and affordable experience for budget-conscious travelers. These accommodations frequently capture the essence of Cordoba's cultural legacy, allowing visitors to fully immerse themselves in the local culture without breaking the bank.

Staying in budget-friendly options does not imply losing quality or convenience. Many of these facilities provide clean and pleasant rooms, helpful staff, and convenient locations, making them excellent for visitors who prefer to spend their money on experiences and activities rather than accommodations.

4.3 Unique Lodging Options

Cordoba offers a variety of unusual and unforgettable lodging options in addition to regular hotels and hostels.

Consider staying at one of Cordoba's beautiful boutique hotels, such as the Balcon de Cordoba. These enterprises frequently occupy old buildings and offer a genuine experience that combines modern comforts with the city's cultural history. Imagine waking up in a room with exposed beams and traditional décor, transported to the past while enjoying modern luxuries.

Another unique alternative is to rent a classic Andalusian apartment or house via services such as Airbnb. This allows visitors to immerse themselves in the local culture, living in Cordoba as if they were locals rather than tourists. With possibilities ranging from quaint apartments in the heart of the city to huge houses in the surrounding countryside, this option offers versatility and a sense of home away from home.

Some accommodations provide stays in ancient buildings, such as convents or palaces, which have been turned into hotels. The Palacio del Pilar, for example, allows guests to sleep within the walls of a

15th-century palace, immersed in centuries of history.

4.4 Booking Tips

Whether you choose a deluxe hotel, a low-cost guesthouse, or a unique lodging alternative, good booking tactics will improve your overall Cordoba experience.

1. Book in Advance: Especially during high seasons or major events, booking your accommodations ahead of time ensures a greater choice and, in some cases, lower pricing.

2. Read Reviews: Make use of online platforms to read reviews from other travelers. Real-world

experiences can provide useful insights regarding the quality and originality of accommodations.

3. Consider Location: Select accommodations based on your planned activities. Staying centrally provides convenient access to attractions, although those wanting a quieter experience may prefer accommodation on the outskirts.

4. Date Flexibility: If you have flexible travel dates, you may be able to get cheaper bargains by modifying your arrival and departure dates to avoid peak periods.

5. Contact Directly: In some circumstances, contacting the accommodation directly can result in tailored offers or additional benefits, particularly when dealing with smaller businesses.

To summarize, Cordoba's hotel alternatives accommodate a wide range of interests and budgets. Whether you like the richness of a luxury hotel, the warmth of a low-cost stay, or the distinctiveness of unorthodox lodging, the city makes sure that your choice of lodging becomes a vital component of your total vacation experience. By assessing your priorities, using booking recommendations, and embracing the range of alternatives available, you can choose the ideal location to stay and make the most of your time in this interesting city.

5. EXPLORING THE CITY

Cordoba, with its rich tapestry of history and culture, invites travelers on a fascinating journey of discovery. From the delicate nuances of its historical districts to the breathtaking architectural marvels and recognizable monuments, the city unfolds like a fairytale, with each page revealing a new aspect of its allure.

5.1 Cordoba's Historical Districts

One cannot properly understand Cordoba without exploring its historical areas. The city's convoluted streets reflect the different civilizations that have left their imprint over the millennia. The Jewish Quarter, also known as Juderia, is a charming enclave with small cobblestone alleyways winding past whitewashed buildings covered with bright flowers. This region preserves Cordoba's medieval atmosphere, providing insight into the daily lives of the city's Jewish community during the Middle Ages.

In contrast, the Alcazar Viejo's lovely squares and patios provide a more easygoing atmosphere. This region is a tranquil refuge, where visitors may escape the hustle and bustle of the city center and experience the splendor of Andalusian architecture in a peaceful atmosphere.

Walking through these ancient districts, one can find hidden squares, tiny artisan shops, and lovely cafes. The beauty is in getting lost in the tangle of alleyways and discovering secret corners that reveal Cordoba's true essence.

5.2 Architectural Marvels

Cordoba is a living witness to the peaceful coexistence of diverse cultures, as evidenced by its architectural marvels. The Mezquita-Catedral, located in the middle of the city, is a masterpiece that seamlessly mixes Islamic and Christian features. The horseshoe arches, beautifully constructed mihrab, and awe-inspiring prayer hall all tell stories of Cordoba's long history as Islamic Spain's capital city. The eventual incorporation of a Renaissance cathedral within the mosque's structure adds another layer of complexity, resulting in a unique blend of architectural styles.

The Alcazar of Cordoba, located adjacent to the Mezquita, is a palace stronghold with rich gardens that reflect Moorish design. The intricate mosaics, the cooling sound of fountains, and the perfume of citrus trees transport visitors to another age, providing a glimpse into the splendor of Cordoba's medieval lords.

A short walk from these wonders leads to the Roman Bridge, a strong testament to Roman engineering that spans the Guadalquivir River. As the sun sets, the bridge transforms into a beautiful scene, with the Mezquita lighted in the background. It's a moment that perfectly captures the everlasting grandeur of Cordoba's architectural legacy.

5.3 Iconic Landmarks

Beyond the architectural marvels, Cordoba is dotted with distinctive sites that add to its personality. The Calahorra Tower, which sits at the far end of the Roman Bridge, serves as a sentinel for the city. This stronghold, which originally acted as a defensive construction, is now home to a museum that provides insights into Cordoba's history and the cultural interactions that helped shape it.

A stroll through the city's main square, the Plaza de la Corredera, gives you a sense of Cordoba's bustling atmosphere. The area, surrounded by colorful facades and energetic eateries, serves as a social focus for both locals and tourists looking to drink up the city's vivid spirit. It's a great place to relax with a cup of coffee or observe folks.

For those interested in Cordoba's recent past, the Cristo de los Faroles is a memorable landmark.

This sculpture of a Christ figure surrounded by lamps represents hope and persistence. When illuminated at night, it serves as a light for both locals and visitors, capturing Cordoba's spiritual soul.

Cordoba's prominent landmarks extend outside the city core. The Palacio de Viana, located in the San Basilio district, has twelve exquisite patios, each with their distinct beauty. These courtyards embody the city's patio gardening culture, with brilliant blooms and beautifully manicured plants creating a sanctuary of tranquility.

In conclusion, experiencing Cordoba is a trip through time and culture, with historical neighborhoods, architectural marvels, and iconic landmarks weaving a centuries-long story. Whether you're drawn to the delicate features of the Mezquita-Catedral, the charm of hidden squares in the Jewish Quarter, or the exuberant energy of Plaza de la Corredera, Cordoba's attractions promise a rich and immersive experience for all visitors. As you walk through the city's streets, each step becomes a discovery, and each monument represents a chapter in Cordoba's enthralling story.

6. NATURAL BEAUTY

Cordoba, well-known for its historical and architectural splendors, is also a city rich in natural beauty. Cordoba's seaside marvels and precisely maintained parks and gardens offer a wonderful blend of urban attractiveness and natural quiet. This book explores the city's natural resources, including coastal panoramas, green parks, and a variety of outdoor activities that invite tourists to experience Cordoba's natural beauty.

6.1 Cordoba's Coastal Wonders

While Cordoba is most known for its internal gems, the city's proximity to the ocean adds to its charm. The Costa del Sol, with its golden beaches and gorgeous Mediterranean waters, is easily accessible from Cordoba, making it a great day trip destination.

Visiting the coast gives a welcome respite from the city's congested surroundings. Marbella, one of the most prominent coastal cities, has magnificent beaches and a bustling promenade packed with restaurants and stores. The route from Cordoba to Marbella is a pleasant one, traveling through picturesque surroundings that shift from the old city to beachfront grandeur.

Further along the coast, the town of Nerja captivates visitors with its famed Balcon de Europa, a viewpoint built on a cliff that provides stunning views of the Mediterranean. The neighboring caves of Nerja, a natural wonder with magnificent stalactite formations, provide a geological twist to the coastal adventure.

Cordoba's coastal marvels offer a retreat for visitors looking for a day of relaxation, beach walks, or aquatic activities. Whether you like the vibrant ambiance of beachside towns or the peace of hidden coves, the Costa del Sol reveals a distinct side of Cordoba's rich nature.

6.2 Parks & Gardens

Green oases and well-manicured gardens provide an escape from Cordoba's hectic metropolitan streets. These parks not only enhance the city's scenic attractiveness, but also provide opportunities for recreation, reflection, and a closer connection to nature.

The Alcazar Gardens, located next to Cordoba's Alcazar, offer a symphony of hues and scents. Fountains, geometrically shaped hedges, and vivid flower beds create a serene setting that matches Alcazar's architectural grandeur. Exploring these gardens is like walking into a live canvas, with each corner revealing a meticulously maintained arrangement.

Parque Cruz Conde, located near the city center, is a popular recreational area enjoyed by both locals and visitors. The park's expansive green lawns, playgrounds, and shaded walks make it ideal for picnics, outdoor activities, and a leisurely afternoon stroll. It's a place where the dynamic energy of Cordoba's city life blends with the soothing effect of nature.

The Jardin Botanico de Cordoba offers a more immersive experience by displaying a broad assortment of flora, with themed gardens reflecting various ecosystems. From the Mediterranean Garden to the Tropical Greenhouse, this botanical garden is both informative and pleasurable. Visitors can explore verdant settings and discover plant species from all around the world.

6.3 Outdoor Activities

Cordoba's natural beauty extends beyond static vistas, encouraging outdoor enthusiasts to participate in a variety of activities that take advantage of the city's surroundings.

The Guadalquivir River, which flows through the heart of Cordoba, provides chances for water-related activities. Kayaking along the river offers a unique view of the city's skyline, including sights of historic landmarks from a peaceful vantage point. Several local firms provide guided kayaking tours, making it accessible to both novices and expert paddlers.

Hiking lovers can explore the Sierra Morena, a mountain range that surrounds Cordoba's northern fringes. Trails wind through lush forests, leading to magnificent overlooks that provide panoramic views of the surrounding area. The Sierra Morena provides a natural sanctuary, allowing trekkers to breathe fresh air and escape the metropolitan rhythm.

Cycling is another popular outdoor sport in Cordoba, with several routes suitable for all ability levels. Cyclists may enjoy a dynamic exploration of Cordoba's natural surroundings, whether on the city's bike trails or in the neighboring countryside.

For those looking for a more calm outdoor experience, the city's parks frequently host yoga sessions, and exercise groups, or simply offer peaceful spaces for meditation and contemplation. These activities not only enhance physical well-being but also provide a peaceful connection with nature amidst the urban chaos.

To summarize, Cordoba's natural beauty is a multifaceted treasure that manifests itself through coastline beauties, finely built parks, and a wealth of outdoor activities. Cordoba welcomes you to embrace its many natural settings, whether you like the peace of botanical gardens, the liveliness of seaside cities, or the dynamic energy of outdoor activities. Exploring the city's green spaces, participating in outdoor activities, or going on a beach vacation all contribute to the story of Cordoba's rich and complex beauty.

7. HIDDEN GEMS

Cordoba, with its layers of history and cultural diversity, hides secrets beyond the well-worn routes of tourist sites. These hidden gems, beloved by residents, inspire interested visitors to venture off the main path and discover the city's lesser-known treasures. From secret locales adored by Cordobas to off-the-beaten-path attractions and unique experiences, this book reveals the hidden gems that add an extra layer of enchantment to Cordoba's tapestry.

7.1 Secret Spots Locals Love

A city's authenticity is typically found in the locations that its citizens know and love. Cordoba, with its kind and welcoming community, has secret sites that people treasure.

Bar Santos, located in Cordoba's Jewish Quarter, is a hidden gem for visitors looking for an authentic flavor of the city's cuisine. Locals frequent this unpretentious tapas eatery, which is well-known for its salmorejo, a typical Andalusian cold soup. The simple décor and welcoming ambiance make it a popular hangout, allowing guests to taste true local cuisine away from the tourist crowds.

For a peaceful respite, the Patios of Viana provide a lesser-known aspect of the Cordobas patio tradition. While the city is most known for its Courtyards Festival in May, the Patios of Viana provide a year-round experience. These twelve patios, each with its distinct charm, highlight the beauty of traditional Andalusian architecture and landscaping. It's a peaceful retreat away from the masses, where you can admire the painstaking care put into these secret courtyards.

Cordoba residents also find solace in the Gardens of La Merced. This beautiful retreat, situated behind the Convento de la Merced, offers a haven of nature and tranquility. With its fountains, shady walks, and brilliant blooms, the gardens provide a peaceful getaway in the center of the city.

7.2 Off-Beaten-Path Attractions

While the Mezquita and Alcazar deserve their place in the spotlight, Cordoba also has lesser-known sights that enchant with their unique appeal.

The Calleja de las Flores, a short lane lined with vivid flowerpots, entices visitors with its stunning beauty. This lovely alley, which is frequently ignored by visitors to the main attractions, provides a picturesque backdrop as well as a moment of tranquility. As you walk along its cobblestone walkway, the aroma of blooms and brilliant colors create a memorable environment.

The Roman Temple, located near the city center, commemorates Cordoba's ancient heritage. Often overlooked by the magnificence of the Mezquita, this well-preserved relic of Roman construction encourages history buffs to explore the city's vast cultural past.

Casa Andalusí, located in the San Basilio area, provides insight into Cordoba's Islamic past. This restored house features the architectural and ornamental aspects of a typical Andalusian dwelling from the 12th century. The intimate atmosphere allows visitors to experience the domestic lives of Cordoba's citizens in a bygone age.

7.3 Unique Experiences

Cordoba goes beyond physical landmarks, providing one-of-a-kind experiences that contribute to the city's rich cultural fabric.

One such experience is attending a Flamenco Tablao. While Flamenco is synonymous with Andalusian culture, Tablaos offers a more intimate and authentic experience. Locals frequent these locations, enjoying the impassioned performances that capture the essence of Flamenco. Engaging with this art form in a smaller environment allows guests to fully experience Flamenco's emotional depth and intensity.

The Feria de los Patios, held in early May, offers a one-of-a-kind opportunity to explore local artistry. This festival celebrates Cordoba's patio tradition, in which inhabitants open up their homes to the public, exhibiting beautifully decorated courtyards. Exploring these private places provides a rare peek into the creativity and dedication that locals put into their patios. The festival also includes live music, traditional dancing, and a lively ambiance that captures Cordoba's cheerful character.

Those who visit the Mercado Victoria can look forward to a gourmet adventure. While not hidden in the usual sense, this bustling food market is a gastronomic paradise. Locals frequent the market to sample a wide range of tapas, exotic cuisines, and local specialties. It's a sensory journey that brings Cordoba's flavors to life, creating a one-of-a-kind and immersive culinary experience.

Finally, Cordoba's hidden beauties offer a side of the city that many casual tourists overlook. These hidden treasures add dimension to a tour around Cordoba, whether it's exploring secret areas cherished by residents, discovering off-the-beaten-path attractions, or immersing oneself in unique experiences. By traveling beyond the well-known attractions, visitors can form a more intimate connection with the city, uncovering its layers of history, culture, and the vivid spirit of its inhabitants.

8. CULTURAL DELIGHTS

Cordoba, a city rich in history and culture, spreads like a cultural tapestry, inviting tourists to immerse themselves in a diverse range of artistic expressions and exuberant celebrations. Cordoba delivers a stimulating experience for visitors eager to discover its cultural treasures, from museums and art galleries that highlight the city's rich legacy to bustling festivals and events that will punctuate the cultural calendar in 2024.

8.1 Museums and Art Galleries

Cordoba's cultural landscape reflects the city's diversified background, and its museums and art galleries preserve this rich tradition.

The Archaeological and Ethnological Museum of Cordoba, located near the Roman Bridge, offers a fascinating tour through the city's past. Artifacts from diverse periods, such as Roman, Visigothic, and Islamic, are meticulously presented, providing insight into the numerous civilizations that have made their mark on Cordoba. The museum's collection serves as a visual narrative, allowing visitors to follow the city's history over time.

For art lovers, the Fine Arts Museum of Cordoba is a treasure trove of Spanish artworks from the Middle Ages to the twentieth century. The museum, located in the Palacio de la Merced, features works by prominent artists such as Velázquez, Goya, and Sorolla. The eclectic collection illustrates the growth of Spanish art, offering a thorough overview of artistic expressions from many times.

The Sephardic House, located in the heart of Cordoba's Jewish Quarter, honors the city's Jewish past. The museum focuses on the history, culture, and contributions of Cordoba's Sephardic Jewish population. Intricate relics, texts, and displays tell the narrative of a once-thriving population behind the city walls.

In addition to these museums, Cordoba has several art galleries, each of which contributes to the city's contemporary artistic scene. The Sala Aires, for example, features works by both local and foreign artists, creating a dynamic environment for creative expression. Exploring these galleries allows visitors to interact with Cordoba's changing cultural identity, where the past and present meet in a lively interaction.

8.2 Festivals and Events in 2024

Cordoba's calendar is full of festivals and events that commemorate the city's cultural richness, allowing visitors to see traditional rituals, enjoy artistic performances, and participate in the dynamic spirit of the community.

The Cordoba Patio Festival, held in May, is a legendary event that transforms the city into a riot of colors and fragrances. Residents open out their private patios, which are decorated with flowers and ornamental items, to the public. The festival is a sensory feast, allowing guests to discover the private beauty of these secret courtyards, interact with the happy proprietors, and admire the exquisite care that went into producing these floral beauties.

For music fans, the Cordoba Guitar Festival in July is a must-see event. This event, held in a variety of historic sites throughout the city, promotes the guitar in all of its forms, from classical to flamenco. Concerts, workshops, and contests bring together musicians and fans, resulting in an immersive experience infused with the beautiful melodies of the guitar.

Cordoba also honors its equine legacy with the Cordoba Horse Fair, held annually in May. The fair features the Andalusian horse, which is known for its grace and beauty. Visitors may watch traditional equestrian displays, and flamenco performances, and enjoy the lively ambiance of the fairgrounds. It's a celebration that encapsulates the spirit of Andalusian tradition, honoring the link between horse and rider with style and grace.

Cordoba's great relationship with music is highlighted by the Festival de la Guitarra, which will take place in July. Beyond guitar performances, the festival features a wide spectrum of musical genres, from jazz to classical. Renowned musicians and young talents come together to create a harmonious celebration of musical variety.

Cordoba is expected to stage a plethora of events and festivals in 2024, all of which will contribute to the community's cultural vibrancy. Whether it's historic processions, contemporary art displays, or gastronomic feasts, the city's calendar reflects a dedication to maintaining its legacy while also embracing the energy of today.

To summarize, Cordoba's cultural joys are a dynamic blend of historical veneration and contemporary expression. Museums and art galleries preserve the city's history, providing views into the various cultures that created its identity. Meanwhile, festivals and events fill the cultural calendar, allowing visitors to experience the vibrant spirit of Cordoba's community. By participating in these cultural activities, visitors can form a stronger bond with the city, admiring not only its architectural marvels but also the complex tapestry of traditions, arts, and celebrations that constitute Cordoba's cultural essence.

9. CULINARY ADVENTURES

Cordoba, a city that whispers stories of history through its cobblestoned streets, is not only a treasure trove of architectural beauties but also a culinary paradise. Cordoba's gastronomy scene develops like a complex tapestry, combining Moorish, Jewish, and Christian elements to produce a distinct and savory experience for anyone willing to explore its culinary offerings. Cordoba's cuisine is a delightful journey of discovery, with culinary hotspots reflecting the city's current feel, classic dishes embodying centuries-old recipes, and exciting food excursions beckoning the adventurous palette.

9.1 Culinary Hot Spots

Cordoba's cityscape is studded with culinary hotspots that demonstrate the diversity and originality of its modern gastronomy scene. The Mercado Victoria, a lively food market near the city center, exemplifies Cordoba's commitment to culinary quality. With its lively ambiance and diverse stalls serving everything from local tapas to international cuisines, the market is a sensory joy for foodies.

The Taberna Luque, located in the heart of the Jewish Quarter, is a culinary delight enjoyed by both locals and visitors. This historic pub captures the essence of Andalusian food, with a menu rich in local tastes. Taberna Luque offers authentic

Cordoba cuisine, including classic salmorejo and flavorful flamenquín dishes.

Bodegas Mezquita, located near the Mezquita-Catedral, offers a contemporary touch on traditional Andalusian cuisine by combining current culinary techniques. The restaurant, housed in a historic building with a gorgeous patio, serves a menu that highlights the region's best ingredients in inventive ways. It's a place where culinary artistry meets Cordoba's gourmet heritage.

La Furgo Trattoria, a hidden gem away from the tourist crowd, is popular among residents. This lovely trattoria charms customers with homemade pasta, wood-fired pizzas, and a welcoming atmosphere. La Furgo Trattoria captures the essence of Cordoba's culinary culture, combining authentic ingredients and a welcoming atmosphere.

9.2 Traditional Dishes

Cordoba's gastronomic identity is profoundly established in its historical tapestry, with traditional dishes honoring the region's rich cultural past. Salmorejo, a cold tomato soup that originated in Andalusia, stands at the vanguard of this culinary legacy. The Cordoban version of salmorejo is well-known for its silky texture and rich flavor, which is sometimes served with hard-boiled eggs and jamón serrano. Locals enjoy this refreshing dish, particularly during the hot summer months.

Flamenquín is a well-known dish in Cordoba. This breaded and fried roll, usually stuffed with ham or pork, represents the luxurious side of Andalusian cuisine. Flamenquín, a traditional Cordoban meal, can be found at many tapas bars and restaurants. It is a robust and tasty option.

Rabo de Toro, or oxtail stew, exemplifies Cordoba's Moorish influence. Slow-cooked until tender, the oxtail is simmered in a thick wine and tomato sauce, resulting in a savory and aromatic delicacy. Rabo de Toro, which is typically eaten with potatoes or rice, is a culinary voyage back in time, providing a taste of the historical flavors that have influenced Andalusian cuisine.

Pastel Cordobés is a dish that celebrates Cordoba's Moorish heritage. This almond and pumpkin-filled pastry, decorated with powdered sugar, originated during the Moorish conquest of the Iberian Peninsula. The exquisite combination of flavors and textures makes it an ideal finale for a traditional Cordoban meal.

9.3 Food Adventures

Culinary adventures in Cordoba go beyond typical cuisine, providing thrilling encounters for the daring palate. Exploring the city's tapas culture is an adventure in itself, with local bars serving up a variety of small meals that highlight the region's culinary prowess. El Churrasco, a classic Cordoban eatery, is well-known for its vast tapas menu, which allows guests to enjoy a range of cuisines in a sociable setting.

A gourmet tour of Cordoba's patios offers an immersive view of the city's gastronomic and architectural legacy. During the Patio Festival in May, locals open their houses to the public, providing not only a visual feast of floral arrangements but also the opportunity to sample homemade cuisine. It's an exceptional opportunity to interact with locals, share tales, and experience the original flavors of Cordoba's home-cooked meals.

Cordoba's culinary narrative revolves around olive oil, a staple of Andalusian cuisine. Visitors can learn about the intricacies of olive oil through tastings and excursions, which range from the fruity aromas of early harvest oils to the strong flavors of mature kinds. Local olive oil mills, such as the Almazaras de la Subbética, welcome visitors to learn about the olive oil production process and participate in tastings that enhance their appreciation for this crucial element.

Cordoba's wine scene also entices lovers to go on a vinicultural trip. The Montilla-Moriles region, near Cordoba, is well-known for its fortified wines, notably the famed Pedro Ximénez. Bodegas like Alvear and Toro Albala provide wine tastings, which provide insights into the region's winemaking traditions as well as the opportunity to sample fine wines that combine nicely with Cordoba's gastronomic delicacies.

To summarize, Cordoba's culinary scene is an intriguing blend of history and innovation, reflecting the city's many cultural influences. Cordoba's culinary delights are a feast for the senses, with places that highlight contemporary ingenuity, classic meals that embody centuries-old recipes, and fascinating eating adventures that encourage exploration. Visitors can actively participate in Cordoba's gastronomic trip by enjoying salmorejo, flamenquín, and tapas pubs and patios.

10. LOCAL LIFESTYLE

Cordoba's charm goes beyond its historical buildings and culinary delights; it is firmly ingrained in the local culture that flows through its small alleys and bustling squares. Understanding and immersing oneself in Cordoba's everyday rhythms is essential for fully understanding the city's soul. Cordoba's local lifestyle is a vibrant mosaic of tradition, conviviality, and contemporary energy, from the vibrant markets and bazaars that serve as the beating heart of local commerce to the cozy cafés and hangout spots where friendships thrive, and the dynamic nightlife that transforms the city after sundown.

10.1 Cordoban Markets and Bazaars

To get a sense of Cordoba's local lifestyle, visit the lively marketplaces and bazaars. The Mercado Victoria, located near the Mezquita, exemplifies the city's rich market culture. This contemporary culinary market is a fusion of flavors, scents, and community spirit. From fresh fruit to gourmet tapas, it's a gathering spot for locals to interact, experience culinary delights, and commemorate the city's rich culinary history.

For a more traditional market experience, the Mercado de la Corredera provides a look into Cordoba's everyday life. This market, housed in a historic building, takes place beneath a grand arcade, creating a wonderful atmosphere. The stalls are brimming with fresh fruits, vegetables, spices, and local products. It's a place where the bustle of Cordoba's business blends with the warmth of interpersonal interactions.

Visitors to Cordoba's ancient Jewish Quarter will come upon the Zoco Municipal, a bazaar that honors the city's history. Craftsmen and craftsmen sell their handmade goods, ranging from leather to ceramics, at a market reminiscent of Andalusia's historic souks. The Zoco Municipal is more than just a marketplace; it embodies the city's craftsmanship and commercial traditions.

10.2 Cafés and Hangout Spots

Cordoba's local lifestyle unfolds gently in its countless cafés and hangout spots, where friends congregate, talks flow, and life settles into a calm rhythm.

Café de la Libertad, a historic café in Cordoba's core, is one example. With its outside patio facing the Plaza de la Libertad, it's a great place for residents to relax with a cup of coffee or a glass of wine. The café's bohemian ambiance, live music, and diverse décor create a welcoming environment that embodies Cordoba's artistic and intellectual culture.

For a more modern atmosphere, the concept store and café Combo the Cult is a popular choice among the younger audience. It is located in the San Basilio district and combines a fashionable shop and a café, offering a handpicked variety of fashion, design, and coffee. It's a place where creative impulses meet and locals get together to celebrate both the visual and culinary arts.

Café El Potro is set in the middle of the historic neighborhood, with the Plaza del Potro serving as a picturesque background. This café, with its vintage décor and outdoor seating, is a favorite among locals looking for a peaceful getaway from the hustle and bustle of the city. It's a spot where time seems to slow down, allowing customers to enjoy their drinks while immersed in Cordoba's historic charm.

10.3 Nightlife & Entertainment

As the sun sets, Cordoba transforms into a dynamic nightlife and entertainment scene that keeps the city alive into the early hours.

The Guadalquivir Riverbanks, notably El Arenal, are bustling with riverside bars and clubs. Locals and visitors alike gather to enjoy a drink, dance to live music, or simply take in the vibrant ambiance. The riverbanks transform into a nightly playground, with the lights of the Mezquita shimmering in the background, creating a magnificent atmosphere.

Cordoba's Flamenco clubs, or tablaos, provide an authentic Andalusian experience. These intimate spaces highlight the passion and intensity of Flamenco performances, with expert dancers, impassioned singers, and virtuoso guitarists taking the spotlight. Tablao Cardenal, located in the heart of the city, is a well-known venue that captivates audiences with real Flamenco performances, offering a cultural immersion into the heart of Andalusian culture.

For those looking for a more leisurely evening, Tendillas Square is a central gathering place surrounded by pubs and cafes. The square, which is decorated with fountains and palm trees, is a favorite place for people-watching and mingling. It's an excellent starting point for a night out in Cordoba, where the friendly atmosphere of the square sets the tone for the evening's festivities.

Cordoba's nightlife is diverse, ranging from jazz clubs to electronic music locations, as the city welcomes modernity. The Sala Metrópolis, housed in a historic theater, is a vibrant venue for concerts, DJ sets, and cultural events. It illustrates Cordoba's capacity to combine its ancient history with modern forms of art and entertainment.

In conclusion, Cordoba's local lifestyle is a combination of heritage and modernity, as evidenced by its markets, cafés, and active nightlife. Visitors can immerse themselves in daily life by wandering around the Mercado Victoria, having coffee at a historic café, or dancing to Flamenco rhythms on the riverbanks. By adopting the local way of life, you not only see the grandeur of Cordoba's architectural marvels, but you also become a part of the city's living, breathing fabric.

11. SHOPPING IN CORDOBA

Cordoba, with its rich historical tapestry and strong local culture, provides a distinctive shopping experience that reflects the city's many influences. Cordoba's shopping scene is a lovely blend of tradition and modernity, with high-end stores catering to sophisticated tastes and lively local markets packed with authentic items. This book takes readers through the city's unique shopping scene, emphasizing high-end boutiques, visiting local markets, identifying the best shopping districts, and providing helpful shopping suggestions for visitors looking to discover Cordoba's retail offers.

11.1 High-end Boutiques

Cordoba's high-end boutiques appeal to visitors looking for elegance, sophistication, and unique treasures. A tour across the city reveals a variety of boutiques featuring both local and international designers, creating a customized shopping experience.

Calle Cruz Conde, Cordoba's high street, is lined with upmarket businesses selling well-known designer labels. Boutiques such as Piamonte and Serrano Manchego promote the most recent fashion trends, selling clothing, accessories, and footwear to discerning clients. These stores not only allow visitors to indulge in high-end fashion, but they also contribute to Cordoba's global atmosphere.

Joyería Tejada offers one-of-a-kind, handcrafted jewelry that exudes elegance. This boutique, located near the Mezquita, features a carefully picked range of jewels designed with precision and artistic flair. Joyería Tejada offers a wide range of jewelry styles, including ornate silver pieces influenced by Cordoba's Moorish past and modern designs.

The Posada del Potro neighborhood, known for its historic elegance, is also home to boutique boutiques that combine heritage with modern aesthetics. Boutiques such as La Tienda de Ana and El Rinconcillo provide a carefully curated range of local workmanship, such as handmade ceramics, leather products, and fabrics. These businesses capture the essence of Cordoba, where traditional creativity meets contemporary sensibilities.

11.2 Local Markets and Souvenirs

Cordoba's local markets offer a lively and unique shopping experience, allowing tourists to immerse themselves in the city's cultural and artisanal traditions. These marketplaces are ideal for individuals looking for one-of-a-kind mementos and traditional handicrafts.

In addition to its gourmet attractions, the Mercado Victoria houses artisan stalls where local craftsmen display their handmade goods. The market's artisan sector offers a variety of unique gifts that capture Cordoba's artistic character, including ceramics, textiles, jewelry, and leather goods.

Visitors to the old Jewish Quarter will meet the Zoco Municipal, a market evocative of traditional souks. This bazaar displays the talents of local craftsmen, who sell handmade items like ceramics, fabrics, and delicate metalwork. The Zoco Municipal is an excellent choice for visitors looking for original souvenirs that reflect Cordoba's historical and cultural heritage.

The Feria de Artesanía de Córdoba is an annual festival of local craftsmanship. This craft festival brings together craftsmen from Cordoba and beyond, showcasing a wide range of handmade products. From traditional pottery and woven carpets to contemporary artworks, the expo offers a complete look at Andalusian workmanship. It's a great opportunity to meet artisans, learn about their processes, and buy one-of-a-kind handmade mementos.

11.3 Best Shopping Districts

Cordoba's top shopping districts provide a wide range of retail experiences, from lovely old alleyways lined with boutique shops to bustling commercial areas catering to a variety of preferences.

The Jewish Quarter, with its small alleyways and whitewashed buildings, is both a historical site and a retail magnet. Calleja de las Flores, embellished with vivid flowerpots, houses a range of modest businesses and boutiques. It's a beautiful street where people can stroll and discover hidden gems.

Cordoba's main shopping street, Calle Cruz Conde, is lined with a mix of high-end boutiques, foreign brands, and local retailers. This commercial center is perfect for those shopping for clothing, accessories, and specialty shops. The street's bustling environment enhances the entire shopping experience.

The Plaza de las Tendillas, a lively center in the heart of Cordoba, is lined with businesses and department stores. This shopping mall has a wide selection of options, including popular brands and local stores. The square's central location makes it an ideal starting point for those wanting to explore Cordoba's retail scene.

The area surrounding the Mezquita and Alcazar offers a mix of history and shopping, with boutique stores and artisan shops. Exploring the neighborhoods near these prominent landmarks allows visitors to mix cultural study with retail therapy, discovering unusual items in historic settings.

11.4. Shopping Tips

Navigating Cordoba's shopping scene is a wonderful experience, and here are a few pointers to help:

1. Explore Off-the-Beaten-Path Stores: While main shopping routes provide a range of possibilities, don't be afraid to venture down side streets and alleys. Many hidden jewels, artisan studios, and unusual boutiques are nestled away in less traveled places.

2. Embrace Local Craftsmanship: Cordoba's artisanal past is visible in its handcrafted items. Look for locally made items including ceramics, leather goods, and textiles. These unique gifts not only have cultural significance but also benefit local craftspeople.

3. Shopping hours in Cordoba may vary from those in other cities. Keep in mind the typical siesta period, when many shops close in the afternoon. Evening shopping is popular, particularly during the warmer months when the city comes alive after dark.

4. Engage with Artisans: When shopping at markets or craft fairs, take advantage of the opportunity to interact with artisans. They frequently have great anecdotes to tell about their

trade, and you may gain insight into the traditional procedures utilized to create their items.

5. Combine commercial with Exploration: Cordoba's commercial districts are frequently linked to historic neighborhoods and attractions. Plan your shopping plan to incorporate stops to explore the city's cultural and architectural marvels.

To summarize, shopping in Cordoba is more than just a transaction; it is an immersion into the city's cultural, artistic, and historical tapestry. Cordoba's retail scene ranges from high-end boutiques to lively markets, reflecting the city's many influences and contemporary vibrancy. Visitors can bring home physical memories of their Cordoban experience by exploring the city's shopping areas, meeting with local artisans, and celebrating the richness of Cordoba's craftsmanship.

12. PLANNING YOUR ITINERARY

Cordoba, with its rich history, cultural tapestry, and different attractions, provides a wealth of experiences for visitors. Creating a well-planned itinerary ensures that you make the most of your stay in this wonderful city. Cordoba has something for everyone, whether you're interested in history, cuisine, or nature. This book will help you organize your schedule by providing sample itineraries for various interests, proposing day trips from Cordoba, and recommendations for traveling with family, friends, or solo.

12.1 Sample Itineraries for Different Interests

History Enthusiast's Itinerary:

Day 1: Morning - Exploring the Historic District

- Begin your day by visiting the Mezquita-Catedral, where you may admire the architectural combination of Islamic and Christian features.

- Walk through the Jewish Quarter, traversing the small lanes and visiting the Synagogue and Casa Andalusí.

Day 1: Afternoon at Alcazar and Calahorra Tower.

- Visit the Alcázar de los Reyes Cristianos and explore its gardens, courtyards, and the medieval stronghold.

- Go to the Calahorra Tower, which houses a museum that tells Cordoba's history and displays Islamic relics.

Day 2: Morning at the Archaeological Museum and Roman Sites

- Spend the morning at the Archaeological and Ethnological Museum, learning about Cordoba's past.

- Visit the Roman Bridge and the adjoining Roman Temple to connect with Cordoba's historic heritage.

Foodie's itinerary:

Day 1: Morning at Mercado Victoria and Breakfast.

- Begin your culinary adventure in Mercado Victoria by sampling local tapas and delicacies.

- Have a leisurely breakfast at one of the wonderful cafés in the historic center.

Day 1: Afternoon Cooking Class and Tapas Tour.

- Attend a traditional Andalusian cooking lesson and learn how to prepare local foods.

- In the evening, go on a tapas tour to sample the various flavors of Cordoba's cuisine.

Day 2: Morning Olive Oil Tour and Tasting.

- Take a tour of a local olive oil mill and learn about the subtleties of this crucial component.

- Participate in an olive oil tasting to appreciate the many flavors and variations.

Nature Lovers' Itinerary:

Day 1: Morning at Gardens of La Merced.

- Start your day by visiting the serene Gardens of La Merced.

- Discover the rich foliage, fountains, and peaceful walks.

Day 1: Afternoon Natural Parks and Outdoor Activities.

- Visit Sierra de Hornachuelos Natural Park for hiking and natural paths.

- Participate in outdoor activities like bird watching or horseback riding.

Day 2: Morning at Cordoba's Coastal Wonders

- Explore Cordoba's coastal districts, enjoying the beaches and seaside landscapes.

- Engage in water activities or simply relax by the Mediterranean.

12.2-Day Trips from Cordoba

Cordoba's proximity to Seville:
- Take a 45-minute train ride to Seville and visit the Alcazar, Plaza de España, and ancient Santa Cruz area.

Medina Azahara Excursion:
- Explore the archeological site of Medina Azahara, an ancient city about 8 kilometers from Cordoba.

Explore the well-preserved ruins and discover its interesting history.

Jaen and Olive Oil Route:
- Visit Jaen, an hour away, to explore the Olive Oil Route. Visit olive oil mills, sample different kinds, and discover the lovely scenery of olive groves.

Carmona's Historic Charm:
- Travel to Carmona, a historic town about 1.5 hours distant noted for its well-preserved Roman and Moorish buildings. Visit Sevilla's Alcázar de la Puerta and take a stroll around the lovely streets.

12.3 Traveling with Family, Friends, or Solo

Traveling with family:

- Participate in family-friendly activities, such as visiting the Zoo de Córdoba or the Botanical Gardens.

- Explore the Alcazar's grounds, which offer a spacious and scenic setting for a family stroll.

Traveling With Friends:

- Plan a tapas night, visiting various bars and sampling a variety of local cuisine.

- See a Flamenco show together and immerse oneself in the passionate rhythms of Andalusian music and dance.

Solo Traveler's Experience:

- Take a walking tour to meet other tourists and learn about the city from a knowledgeable guide.

- Go to a local café and strike up talks with people while taking in the atmosphere of Cordoba's communal places.

General Tips for Every Traveler:

1. Flexible Planning: While a rough itinerary is necessary, allow for spontaneity and exploration. Cordoba's appeal is typically found in surprises.

2. Respecting Siesta Hours: Keep in mind that certain shops close in the afternoon for their traditional siesta hours. Plan your activities accordingly.

3. Local Transportation: Familiarize yourself with Cordoba's public transit system, which includes buses and trains, for easy and affordable travel within the city and to adjacent places.

4. Language Considerations: Although many people speak English, learning a few basic Spanish phrases might help you have a better experience and engage with others.

5. Cultural etiquette includes respecting local customs and traditions, especially when visiting religious places. Dress modestly when entering churches or mosques.

Finally, when arranging your Cordoba itinerary, make sure to personalize it to your interests and tastes. Cordoba has something for everyone, whether you want to learn about history, eat delicious food, explore nature, or go on a day trip. Consider your travel companions and be receptive to the city's possibilities to create a memorable and rewarding vacation through the heart of Andalusia.

13. PRACTICAL INFORMATION

Embarking on a visit to Cordoba is an exciting concept, and having a smooth experience requires understanding the practicalities of traveling to a new location. This thorough book gives practical recommendations to enhance your Cordoba journey, from putting safety and health first to navigating currency exchange and embracing local culture. Whether you're a seasoned tourist or a first-time adventurer, these tips will help you have a wonderful and worry-free stay in this enchanting Andalusian city.

13.1 Safety and Health Information

Cordoba, like any other city, values the safety and well-being of its citizens and visitors. Being knowledgeable of local safety requirements and health concerns is critical for a safe and happy trip.

1. Health Tips:

- Medical Facilities: Learn about the locations of Cordoba's hospitals and medical clinics. The city has contemporary healthcare facilities, including the Hospital Universitario Reina Sofia.

- Pharmacies: Pharmacies (Farmacias) are widely distributed and can help with common ailments. It's important to note that some prescriptions may have different names in Spain, so keep a list of generic names with you.

- Emergency Services: The emergency number for medical assistance in Spain is 112. English-speaking operators are available, ensuring clear communication during an emergency.

2. General Safety Tips:

- Protect Your Property: Cordoba, like any other tourist site, may experience incidents of petty theft. Keep your valuables secure, wear anti-theft bags, and exercise caution in busy situations.

- Street Smart: Although Cordoba is considered safe, use common sense. Avoid poorly lighted areas at night, and be aware of your surroundings.

- Local conventions: Follow local conventions and traditions. In a social context, it is usual to greet someone with a handshake or a kiss on both cheeks.

13.2 Emergency Contacts

Being informed of emergency contacts is critical for prompt response and support in unexpected situations.

1. In a medical emergency, dial 112 for quick assistance.

2. Police: Dial 112 in the event of a criminal situation or an emergency that requires police action.

3. The Tourist Police (Policía Turística) can be contacted at 091. They specialize in serving travelers and can communicate in several languages.

13.3 Currency, Banking, and Payment Options

Understanding the local currency, banking facilities, and preferred payment methods makes financial transactions easier throughout your time in Cordoba.

1. Currency and Banking:

- Euro (€): Spain's official currency is the euro. Make sure you have enough cash for small purchases and businesses that may not accept cards.

- ATMs: Cordoba has a large number of ATMs, particularly in business areas. Inform your bank about your travel dates to avoid any problems with card transactions.

- Bank Hours: Banks in Cordoba are open from 8:30 a.m. to 2:30 p.m., Monday through Friday. Some may close early on Fridays.

2. Payment methods:

- Credit/Debit Cards: Cordoba accepts most major credit and debit cards. Notify your bank about your travel dates to avoid card problems.

- Contactless Payments: Many businesses, including public transit, now accept contactless payments for extra convenience.

13.4 Sustainable Tourism Practices

Cordoba's rich cultural and natural legacy promotes responsible and sustainable tourism practices.

1. Eco-friendly initiatives:

- Public Transportation: Use public transportation, such as buses or trains, to lessen your carbon footprint.

- Walking and Biking: Explore the city on foot or by bike, minimizing your environmental effect while immersing yourself in Cordoba's beauty.

2. Cultural and Environmental Respect:

- Garbage Disposal: Use proper garbage disposal methods. Many communities have recycling bins, and reducing single-use plastics is encouraged.

- Respect Natural Sites: When visiting natural areas or parks, use authorized routes and respect the flora and wildlife.

13.5 Useful Websites and Applications

Leveraging technology improves your trip experience, and Cordoba has a variety of websites and apps to help with navigation, information, and exploration.

1. Websites:

- Cordoba Tourism Official Website: The official tourism website of Cordoba gives detailed information about attractions, events, and practical details for visitors.

- Renfe (Spanish Railways): The Renfe website is an excellent source of train schedules, ticket bookings, and travel information.

2. Apps:

- Renfe Cercanías app: Get real-time information about local train schedules and routes.

- Google Maps: A fantastic resource for navigating the city, discovering attractions, and planning journeys.

13.6 Local Customs and Etiquette

Embracing local customs and etiquette improves your cultural immersion in Cordoba.

1. Greeting Customs:
- Handshakes and Kisses: In social situations, greetings frequently include a handshake or a kiss on both cheeks. Adapt to the degree of familiarity with the individual.

2. Dinner Etiquette:

- Meal Times: Spaniards usually eat a late lunch (about 2 PM) and dinner (around 9 PM). Restaurants may be less crowded if you eat later.

- Tipping: Tipping is common, and rounding up the amount or leaving an extra 5-10% is welcomed.

3. Respecting Cultural Space:

- Mosques and Churches: When visiting religious buildings like the Mezquita, dress modestly and avoid loud conversations to retain the space's solemnity.

13.7 Useful Phrases and Language Tips

While many people in Cordoba know English, attempting to communicate in Spanish is encouraged and can improve your encounters.

1. Basic Phrases:

Hello: Hola

Thank you: Gracias

Please: Por favor

Excuse me / Sorry: Perdón / Lo siento

Goodbye: Adiós

2. Language Tips:

- Learn Local Phrases: Learn a few basic Spanish phrases to improve conversation and demonstrate respect for the local language.

- Translation applications: Use translation applications to help you when you encounter a language barrier.

Finally, this practical advice is intended to make your visit to Cordoba not only delightful but also logistically and culturally adaptable. You can make the most of your time in this picturesque Andalusian city by putting safety first, learning about local customs, and employing technology. Cordoba, with its warm welcome and numerous offerings, awaits your exploration, and these useful tips will help you make the most of your trip through its historic streets and cultural wonders.

14. CORDOBA IN 2024: WHAT'S NEW AND NOTEWORTHY

As 2024 approaches, Cordoba remains a vibrant city that smoothly blends its rich historical legacy with modern advancements. Whether you're a repeat visitor or exploring the city for the first time, staying up to date on new developments and emerging trends improves your experience. This guide delves into what's new and notable in Cordoba, covering recent developments, forthcoming projects, trend shifts, and frequently asked questions that capture the essence of this lovely Andalusian treasure.

14.1 Recent Developments and Upcoming Projects

Cordoba, like many historic cities, is adapting to accommodate the needs of modern visitors while maintaining its cultural identity.

1. Revitalizing Historic Districts:

- Alcazar restorations: The ongoing restorations of the Alcazar de los Reyes Cristianos aim to improve visitor experiences. The project will improve accessibility, restore historic components, and create interactive exhibits.

- Jewish Quarter Restoration: The historic Jewish Quarter is being meticulously restored to maintain its architectural character. Cobblestone streets, facades, and squares are being refurbished to preserve the district's character.

2. Infrastructure Enhancements:

- Transportation Hub: Plans are underway to build a contemporary transportation hub that will integrate bus and train services to increase city connectivity and make travel easier for visitors.

- Smart City Initiatives: Cordoba is embracing smart city technology to improve urban living. Initiatives include enhanced public Wi-Fi, smart traffic management systems, and digital services for both residents and visitors.

3. Cultural Collaborations and Events:

- International Art Exhibitions: Cordoba is becoming a hotspot for international art exhibitions, with well-known artists displaying their works in partnership with local galleries. This cultural interchange enhances the city's artistic landscape.

- Expanded Festival schedule: The city's festival schedule is expanding to incorporate a variety of ethnic festivals, promoting inclusivity and highlighting Cordoba's eclectic background.

14.2 Trends and Changes in City

Cordoba's dynamic nature is reflected in the city's changing trends, which determine its identity and attraction.

1. Technology-Infused Tourism:

- Augmented Reality Tours: Tech-savvy tourists can enjoy augmented reality tours to help them explore historical locations. This interactive experience offers virtual insights into the city's history, supplementing the standard tour style.

- Digital Cultural Experiences: Museums and historical sites are merging digital elements to provide interactive displays and virtual reality experiences that transport visitors across time.

2. Sustainable Practices:

- Green Initiatives: Cordoba is implementing sustainable measures, ranging from eco-friendly transportation to more green spaces. Visitors can expect programs that promote ethical tourism and environmental conservation.

- Farm-to-Table Dining: There is an increasing emphasis on local, sustainable cuisine. Restaurants are cooperating with local farmers, highlighting regional produce, and implementing environmentally friendly practices into their operations.

3. A blend of modern and traditional architecture:

- Contemporary Architectural Additions: While Cordoba retains its traditional charm, modern architectural components are elegantly blended. New structures enhance the cityscape without overshadowing its prominent landmarks.

- Adaptive Reuse Projects: The adaptive reuse trend continues, with old buildings repurposed into boutique hotels, galleries, and cultural spaces. This method retains the city's past while meeting current demands.

4. Inclusive Cultural Programming:

- diversified Art Exhibitions: Cordoba is moving toward a more diversified and inclusive cultural landscape. Art exhibitions and events highlight a diverse range of artistic expressions, reflecting the city's receptivity to new cultural influences.

- Multilingual Services: As part of their efforts to attract a worldwide audience, several businesses are improving multilingual services. English-friendly signage, guided tours, and information are becoming more common.

14.3 Frequently Asked Questions

Addressing typical questions before visiting Cordoba in 2024 can provide important insights.

1. Q: Is Cordoba accessible to tourists with restricted mobility?

A: There have been efforts to improve accessibility in Cordoba. Many attractions, including the Mezquita, Alcazar, and museums, include ramps and other accessibility features. However, it is best to examine specific accessibility features in advance and plan accordingly.

2. Q. When is the ideal time to visit Cordoba?

A: Spring (April to June) and early fall (September to October) are considered the ideal seasons to visit Cordoba. The weather is nice, and outside activities are delightful. However, these are popular times, so preparing ahead is advised.

3. Q: Are there any new food trends in Cordoba?

A: Cordoba's culinary scene is developing, with an emphasis on sustainable and locally sourced ingredients. Farm-to-table eating is gaining popularity, and chefs are experimenting with new dishes influenced by traditional Andalusian flavors.

4. Q: Can I use public transit easily in Cordoba?

A: Yes, Cordoba has an effective public transit system that includes buses and trains. The city is also pedestrian-friendly, making it convenient to explore on foot. Consider getting a transportation card for convenience.

5. Q: Are there limits on photography at historic sites?

A: Most outdoor settings allow photography, however some sites, particularly religious ones, may have restrictions. It is advisable to follow any signage or instructions posted at each location.

6. Q: How can I take part in local cultural events?

A: Keep an eye on the city's event calendar, which lists festivals, art exhibitions, and cultural activities. Many activities are available to the public, and participating adds a distinct dimension to your Cordoba experience.

7. Q: Are there any choices for day trips from Cordoba?

A: Yes, Cordoba's excellent location enables great day trips. Consider visiting Seville, Medina Azahara, Jaen, or Carmona for a wide variety of experiences. Trains and buses provide convenient transportation between these locations.

Finally, Cordoba in 2024 portrays a city in transition, combining its ancient attractiveness with modern achievements. Recent advancements, developing trends, and solutions to commonly asked questions provide an overview of what visitors might expect. Cordoba, in the heart of Andalusia, continues to evolve, welcoming inquiry and discovery, whether you're interested in technical advancements, ecological practices, or a rich tapestry of cultural encounters.

15. CONCLUSION

As our tour of Cordoba comes to an end, it's clear that this lovely city is a tapestry woven with threads of history, culture, and modernization. Cordoba's story is told via every cobblestone and architectural marvel, from the magnificent Mezquita to the bustling alleyways of the Jewish Quarter. In this final piece, we'll highlight Cordoba's ageless allure and provide ideas to make your visit unforgettable.

15.1 Recap of Cordoba's Allure

Cordoba, known as a seaside beauty, exemplifies the alluring mix of influences that have molded its identity.

1. Historical Splendor: The Mezquita-Catedral, a masterpiece of Moorish and Christian architecture, represents the city's rich history. Walking through its enormous interior, which features horseshoe arches and exquisite decorations, transports tourists to a bygone era when Islamic and Christian civilizations coexisted.

2. The historic neighborhoods, from the Jewish Quarter to the Alcazar, provide a voyage through the past. Cobblestone streets, whitewashed buildings, and hidden squares showcase the city's ageless appeal.

3. Natural and Cultural Harmony: Cordoba's coastline beauties, parks, and gardens showcase a balance of nature and culture. The Gardens of La Merced offer tranquil sanctuaries, while the

Mezquita's courtyards highlight the grandeur of Islamic garden design.

4. Cordoba's food culture celebrates history while still being innovative. The city's gastronomic offerings are extensive, ranging from tapas at local bars to farm-to-table experiences.

5. Cordoba's recent developments, such as the Alcazar renovations and smart city initiatives, demonstrate the city's commitment to conserving its legacy while moving forward. The city's cultural calendar, burgeoning festival lineup, and collaborations with foreign artists all highlight its lively present and future.

15.2 Tips for a Memorable Visit

Consider these recommendations to make your visit to Cordoba memorable and seamless:

1. Plan Your Itinerary: Cordoba provides a wide range of experiences, from historical investigations to culinary pleasures. Plan your itinerary around your interests, including must-see landmarks while leaving room for surprises.

2. Embrace Local Customs: Cordoba's warmth extends beyond its climate to its residents. Embrace local norms, such as a warm handshake or the usual siesta routine. Respecting local norms improves your cultural immersion.

3. Explore Beyond the Main Attractions: While the Mezquita and Alcazar are indisputably recognizable, make time to discover hidden gems. Wander through lesser-known streets, connect with residents, and experience the allure of Cordoba's off-the-beaten-path attractions.

4. Stay Up to Date with Recent Developments: Cordoba is always evolving, with ongoing renovations and cultural activities. Stay up to date on recent changes and forthcoming projects to help you better understand the city's present and future.

5. Capture Moments, Respect Spaces: Cordoba's beauty is best appreciated with your eyes, although documenting moments is natural. When photographing, be aware of your surroundings,

especially in religious or historic sites where silence and respect are essential.

6. Try Local Delicacies: Cordoba's food scene is an adventure unto itself. Enjoy native dishes such as salmorejo and flamenquín. Visit local markets and restaurants to sample the unique flavors of Andalusian cuisine.

7. Stay Connected and Navigate Efficiently: Use technology to improve your experience. Useful apps for navigating the city include Google Maps and local transit apps. Stay informed about local events and news by visiting government websites and following social media accounts.

8. Engage with Locals: Cordobans are proud of their city and its traditions. Engage in discussion

with locals, whether at a café, market, or cultural event. Their observations and recommendations might make your journey more personal.

Finally, Cordoba welcomes you to experience not only its historical wonders but also its vibrant present and the promise of its future. As you explore the exquisite arches of the Mezquita, stroll through the historic districts, and experience the aromas of Andalusian food, you become a part of Cordoba's ongoing story. May your visit be full of unforgettable experiences, cultural discoveries, and the timeless allure that marks this coastal jewel in the heart of Andalusia.

Printed in Great Britain
by Amazon